Festive sparkles

How bright and sparkly can you make your decorations?

Chilly penguins

Which baby penguin has lost her woolly hat?

Christmas trail

Can you help Santa's reindeer find his way to the chimney?

Jolly elf

Find the stickers to make the elf's face. Does he look jolly?

Party pals

Can you draw lines between the matching party pals?

Snowy day

Can you find the stickers to decorate the snowy day?

Reindeer Sam

Poor Sam is missing an antler! Can you draw it for him?

Christmas surprises

How shiny and colorful can you make these presents?

Santa's stockings

Santa is on his way, so hang up the stocking stickers!

Candy canes

Can you make this candy cane as striped as the others?

Festive treats

Can you circle the gingerbread men with your crayon?

Holly and berries

These holly leaves need berries! Can you find the stickers?

Sparkly tree

Add stickers to make the tree sparkle, and presents too!

Peter Penguin

Peter wants to be really colorful. Can you help him out?

All wrapped up

Can you draw lines between the matching presents?

Mountain trail

Which trail will lead skier Bob to his friend Anna?

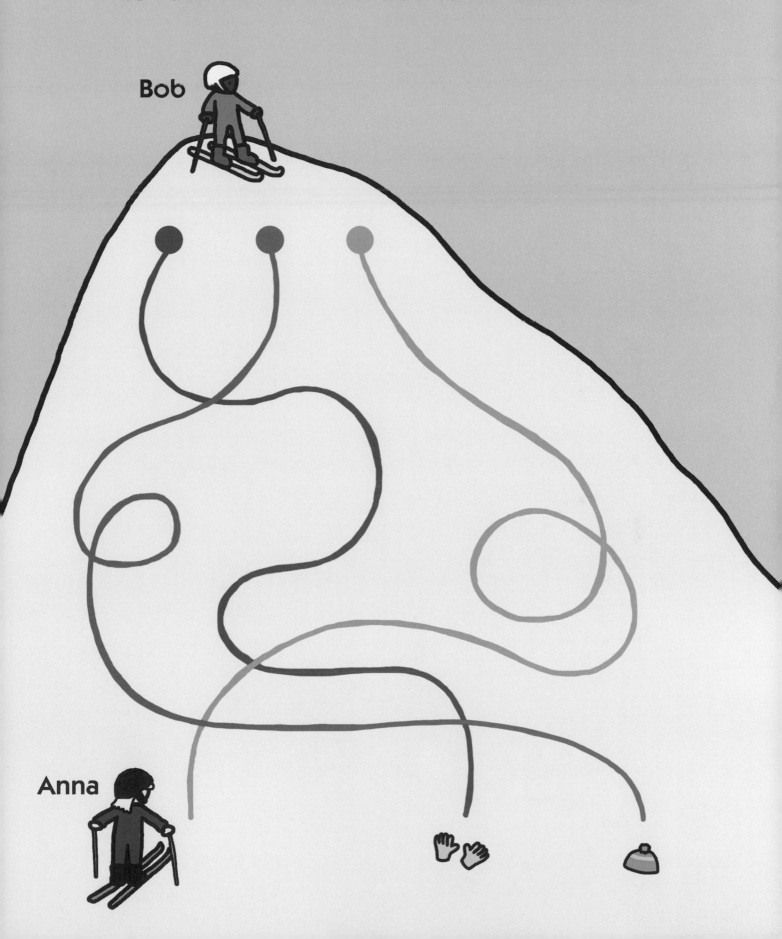

Santa's sleigh ride

Decorate the sky with stickers. Who's pulling the sleigh?

Frosty family

Find the stickers to make Mom, Dad, and little Tim look great.

Speedy skaters

Which ice skater has lost his skates?

Christmas carols

Can you give these carolers colorful hats?

Festive cards

Find the stickers to make these Christmas cards really festive!

Santa's workshop

How many yellow balls can you see in the workshop?

Counting stockings

How many striped stockings can you count?

Smiling Santa

Find the stickers to give Santa a happy face.

Christmas star

Connect the dots, then color in the Christmas star.

Noisy bells

Which bell has a blue ribbon?

Polar pals

Which polar pals are playing in the icy water?